Day 01 – Rekindling the Light

Isaiah 9:2 Those who were walking in darkness have now seen a great light; to the people abiding in the land of lifeless shadows, a new light has come.

CCenturies back, when there were no electric lights, people would bring their very own lamps to night events at their churches. Whenever an evening time praise service was held, households would certainly sit together in their own assigned seat as well as one member would certainly be the caretaker of the light or holder of the light throughout the service.

The entire church would be lit up as people thronged together to worship God, however if a family members was missing out on, their church bench would not just be vacant, there would additionally be an area of dimness because part of the church. The entire parish would certainly know who was missing, so the church seniors would certainly seek the family members out throughout the next week to see if disease or injury had maintained them away from praise.

If individuals stopped coming to church completely, after that those locations of the sanctuary would be dark and also dark. The prayer at the church would certainly continue, however there would certainly constantly be a joyless darkness in that seat up until the household came back or a brand-new family members replaced them

I have actually been a priest for almost 25 years as well as throughout that time I've seen a number of families and friends involve, and go from church in both Scotland as well as the USA. When the delight of worship and also the gladness of confidence diminish in the soul of a person, it is in some cases very tough to rekindle the light of Christ that when was there.

The period of Advent and also the party of Xmas give our churches terrific possibilities to connect to friends and families who have been missing out on from worship for some time. We can favorably use this time around of year to invite them back right into the faith area. If we are truly grateful to see them and also connect to them in a happy way, after that probably the happiness of faith will be revived in their lives.

As we start this trip of Introduction, let's connect and also invite the people that we know in our communities to come as well as discover the pleasure of the Good News through the Xmas solutions, songs, and fellowship chances that we offer from our churches at this fantastic time of the year

Prayer: *Lord Jesus, You are the Happiness Bringer to the whole world and also there are people in our lives that need to reconnect with Your Holy Spirit. We hope that You will provide us numerous chances to*

invite them to praise You this Xmas. Assist us to reach out to them and also allow them to reach back to You. In Your Holy Name, we hope Amen.

Back to Contents

Day 02 – Lights, Cords, and Wires – O My!

***Psalm 116:3** Death's cords entangled me, and the fear of the grave came over me; I was deeply anxious and troubled.*

The beginning of Advent usually suggests that I have to install the Xmas lights outside my home. Each year, I have to disentangle the eco-friendly cords as well as check the bulbs. It's really time consuming, but two years ago I considered something really wise. When it was time to take the lights down, I rolled the cords up thoroughly and examined the light bulbs prior to I placed them in a storage space bag. I was established not to undergo the same twisted mess last Xmas.

However, as the Scottish poet Robert Burns once composed, 'the best laid systems of computer mice as well as guys gang aft agley'. When I tried the lights in 2014, just half of the cables were functioning. As I attempted to discover the broken bulbs, the wires ended up being twisted extremely swiftly. Despite all of that cautious packing as well as pre-planning, I was no far better off. So I threw them all in the trash and also purchased brand-new lights-- lights that mention on the box 'if one goes out, the rest will stay on.' I really feel better concerning that, although there's a concern in my mind which is currently pestering me: what takes place if 2 lights head out?

When King David wrote about the cables of fatality entangling him, he was expressing his beliefs in a pre-Christian age. Fatality frightened David and also his people because there was no hope of eternal life. The Jews of David's time believed that when they passed away, all of their souls went to Sheol, the land of darkness. When there, it was only a matter of time before their spirits disappeared completely into oblivion.

Fortunately, we are Brand-new Testament individuals, so the cables of death can no more entangle us completely. We have a hope in Jesus that will not pass away, neither will certainly it relapse by fatality. When we place our hopes, hearts, as well as beliefs in Him, we are conserved forever. This is fortunately of the Scripture; this is the grateful tidings of great joy that we will usually hear taught throughout Introduction and Christmas.

Prayer: Lord Jesus, we thanks for Your triumph over fatality and dying. We happily applaud You for offering us the glorious possibility to be rejoined and restored to God after fatality. You are the One True and also Living Hero. You are the Only Method to immortality. In Your Holy Name, we happily hope. Amen.

Back to Contents

Day 03 – Embracing Advent

Psalm 115:2   Why does the world say, "Where is their God?"

Q: What's the most effective way to keep Christ in Christmas?
A: Go to church on Sundays.

It astonishes me that individuals that complain Xmas just isn't the same, never ever appear to link their spiritual vacuum with their lack of presence at Church prayer. If they are bombarded with business stress for well over 60 days, then they are bound to be mentally as well as mentally bewildered, specifically if they do not take time out to be with the Lord and His people throughout the Season of Advent.

For many years, I have actually regretfully watched young moms and dads exhaust themselves emotionally as well as financially in order to make Xmas perfect for their youngsters. I have actually seen families obtain agitated as well as fight over information concerning who is hosting Christmas dinner. And also I have actually discovered beleaguered workers and also sales people, who are virtually eliminating themselves in order to enhance their numbers throughout the last month of the year. In the midst of all this stress, it's a lot simpler to allow go of God and misread of the whole celebration.

The Church prepares us for Xmas in purposeful, standard, as well as classic ways. The 4 Sundays in Advent are prayer cars to bring us closer to God in peaceful, valuable, as well as precious means. Instead of questioning what Christmas is everything about and turning it right into a headache, we honestly and just need to get with God's program as well as make Development a spiritual journey where we refocus our lives on Christ.

Celebrating our confidence at Xmas is constantly easy, however as usual we make it made complex. We do not need to place Christ back right into Christmas; He is currently there. We need to place ourselves back right into Christ. His Church gives us that wonderful opportunity every Sunday.

Prayer: Lord Jesus, maintain us from the relentless busyness of Christmas as well as lead us to the tranquility of God's Kingdom. Shield us from going overboard in order to please other individuals. Enable us to make as well as require time to please You. Offer us a heart to be in praise on Sundays and open our hearts to Your Divine Presence. In Your Spiritual Name, we all the best pray. Amen.

<u>Back to Contents</u>

04 – Heart of the Holidays

Galatians 1:11   ***Know this, good people, the Gospel***   ***that I preach is not a myth made up by men.***

There are so many fables as well as tales, custom-mades as well as events affixed to our present celebrations of Christmas that it is occasionally tough to identify what is genuine, important, and also true. We invest so much energy and also effort in advertising, upholding, as well as supporting Xmas traditions that we frequently neglect the basic Gospel message at the heart of our vacations.

Most of the things that we do around this time around of year have really no Gospel link to the remarkable birth of Christ. We get so wrapped up with wrapping gifts up, that we miss God's message to the world which is this: we can experience eternal hope, the forgiveness of transgressions, as well as the pledge of eternal peace with God via Jesus.

We can make ourselves ill with the burdens that we position upon ourselves Christmas We can exhaust ourselves mentally by trying to make everything excellent for everyone else. Rather than enabling Christ to be the Problem Holder of our worries and also the Perfecter of our peace, we busily fight our means via the industrial rush and enable peer stress to dictate our lives.

Christmas was never ever indicated to be like that. The Holy Mass of Christ was intended to be a spiritual time when we allowed Jesus to be the Light of our globe and also the Healer of our sadness. He pertained to show us that we can be conveniently deluded which we commonly trick ourselves with our active means. We truly need Him at this special time, not just to conserve us from our transgressions, however likewise to conserve us from ourselves.

The gladness and benefits of the Scripture at Christmas is a marvelous God-given possibility when we can truly experience a little of the joys of Paradise right here on Earth with inviting Christ right into our hearts and also residences. Besides, when whatever is said and also done and our finite lives wane, it will not be the myths, custom-mades, as well as practices of Christmas that will certainly obtain us right into God's Timeless visibility; it will only be Jesus Christ as our Hero, Lord, as well as King that can do that for us.

Prayer: Lord Jesus, as we progress right into another period of food, celebrations, fables and movies which will certainly stress our financial resources, remind us that belief in You and also real fellowship with God are one of the most integral parts of Christmas. Maintain us from straining our lives and also enjoyed ones with trinkets as well as tinsel, delusions and decorations that have no everlasting value. Remind us that You are the Heart of our holidays as well as the Facility of our parties. In Your Holy Name, we hope. Amen.

<u>Back to Contents</u>

5 – Musical Windows

Psalm 108:3   In the midst of the nations, I will praise You, O LORD; among all peoples, I will glorify You.

I enjoy this time of year, specifically the weeks that lead up to Christmas. Despite where I go, I hear Christmas music as well as carols anywhere. Christianity is a vocal singing confidence as well as I like to think that the tunes and hymns we sing at Christmas are the musical home windows of the church to our neighborhoods.

I recognize that some individuals believe that there's too much commercialism at this time of year which the Spirit of Xmas is lost in an array of indulging, fables, and fun. I made use of to assume like that, however the extra I experience Introduction as well as Christmas, the much more I recognize the power of Manifestation and also the real Presence of Christ worldwide.

Each year we sing of Christ's birth amongst the nations. Every Xmas someone is genuinely touched by the thankful tidings of tranquility as well as pleasure. Every carol has the power to move the hearts of people, that may have separated themselves from church, as well as bring them back to happily commend the Lord. We see this in fact occurring in Christmas Eve prayer services worldwide. That's why they are so crowded. Individuals are attracted to our confidence with the remarkable tunes that we sing as well as dip into this moment of year.

So between now as well as December 25th, I'll be vocal singing, playing, as well as paying attention to as several Xmas carols as I can. My hope is that someone else will certainly hear them as well as find God's happiness to the globe.

Prayer: *Lord Jesus, we offer You thanks for this Development Period when lots of people across the nations happily sing of Your glorious birth. Thanks for the musicians and singers that will motivate, delight, and also please us with their talented gifts as well as songs this Christmas. In Your Holy Name, we joyfully hope. Amen.*

Back to Contents

6 – Sing to The Lord

Zephaniah 3:17 The LORD God is with you and can save you mightily. He delights greatly in you, seeking to pacify you with His love, while He also rejoices over you with singing.

I can bear in mind someone asking me why Christians sing so frequently in their churches. It puzzled him that we spend so much time in worship using songs as well as songs to communicate our appreciation and petitions. "If you cut out the songs," he stated, "every person would certainly get out at 11.30 AM. It wouldn't make any distinction to God. He's only interested in your prayers anyway.".

Clearly, he or she hadn't check out the Scriptures. It has lots of tracks as well as is composed lyrically. The scriptures are suggested to be sung--joyfully as in the Psalms, or dolefully as in Lamentations; noisally like the Angels on the hill, or silently like Mary offering praise to God.

There's also a knowledgeable in bible, the one that we have today, which informs us that God Himself suches as to sing! Songs is an indispensable part of creation, heaven, and also salvation. Song is a sacred automobile of how we approach God, confess to Him, as well as praise His glorious Name. If we were to get songs from our worship, if we were to get rid of all vocal singing, we would be entrusted something tedious, droll, as well as unfeeling.

Songs captivates our hearts as well as gets in touch with our spirits, to ensure that we might mystically get in touch with God. Eventually, when all of His Son's fans are collected in endless time, we will certainly hear one of the most gorgeous voice and the most gorgeous singing in all production, because that will certainly be the sacred moment when God sings and also rejoices with those who are conserved.

Prayer:
Sing to the Lord a cheerful song,.
Raise your hearts, your voices elevate
To us His thoughtful gifts belong,.
To Him our tracks of love and appreciation. John Samuel Bewley Monsell

Back to Contents

7 – Christian Contenders

Philippians 1:27b-28a I will know that you stand firmly in a united spirit, fearlessly contending for the Gospel faith to those who oppose you.

Like most children, I was harassed at institution by numerous people who enjoyed to intimidate me on a daily basis. They would run across me on the football area and journey me up intentionally, or they would gang up on me in a quiet edge and also look for to frighten me.

It obtained so negative that I didn't want to go to school. My qualities plunged and rather than remaining in the top ten group of my class, I sank practically to the bottom. My mama intended to go as well as encounter my day-to-day oppressors, yet I told her not to as that would have shamed me much more. She wasn't mentally fit anyhow, so I didn't believe that she could make any kind of distinction.

After that one early morning during recess, equally as the harasses were involving obtain their typical sadistic pleasure out of intimating me, my mommy appeared out of the blue. She vocally tore into them and publicly humiliated them. As I watched their faces get red with shame, I recognized that they were simply youngsters like me. My mama provided a dressing down and also the other youngsters in the school play area applauded her on. I presume that a few of the other kids had additionally been harassed by them.

Afterwards event, points got better. I wasn't terrified anymore and also soon went back to the top ten pupils of my course. The harasses' regime of fear was ended as well as my mom came to be the heroine of my heart. Sadly, madness as well as schizophrenia would certainly remove the incident from her mind, but also although it has been greater than forty years because the event happened, I still admire her wherefore she did for me that day. She educated me what incarnation was all about which her real presence in the heart of my school world altered everything for the better.

These days, Christians are contending for the Gospel in the face of mistreatment, harassment, imprisonment, and also death in lots of lands. Their unflinching faith is a living testimony to the truth of the Gospel and also the version of Jesus Christ worldwide. Society sometimes seeks to reduce Christianity and also make it irrelevant. Nonetheless, the a lot more that we are philosophically as well as socially opposed, the a lot more real Christians appear to compete for the confidence of the Scripture and also defend Christ's divine words. With Christ among us, we will certainly not be harassed, scolded, or oppressed.

Prayer: *Lord Jesus, confidence is a precious present as well as one that the world seriously needs. Throughout the Planet, Your Church and also Your people are being made to really feel insignificant and also unimportant. We are told that we are intolerant by intolerant individuals. We are considered as being reactionary by those that strongly respond to Your teaching. We are embarrassed as well as pestered throughout the world by brazen bullies and godless federal governments. Assist and also equip us to contend for the Scripture, equally as our bros as well as sisters in our confidence did so lengthy ago. In Your Sacred as well as Holy Name, we hope. Amen.*

Back to Contents

8 – Hopes and Fears

Job 23:16 God has made me faint hearted; I am terrified of the Almighty One.

I sympathize with Work of the Old Testament. He was living at once when individuals thought that individual pain as well as suffering happened since God was upset with them. This implied that any kind of disaster was clouded with a scary concern that God was penalizing individuals. Any kind of illness or illness, any type of obstacle or obstacle was viewed as an indication of God's rage. Just repentance and sacrifice can suffice to calm God. Only humbleness as well as self-reproach could placate the Almighty.

Give thanks to God then that we are Brand-new Testament people! We are no longer bound by those primeval fears. Christ has actually entered into the globe to inform us not to be afraid. Christ has given the supreme sacrifice for every one of our mistakes and sins. The danger of magnificent penalty is no longer to be dreaded. Instead of being frightened of God, we are attracted to Him via the love as well as elegance of Jesus Christ.

Out of the 6.5 billion individuals on this planet, concerning 5 billion live under the spiritual fear of God's wrath. They are frightened of plagues as well as famines, battles as well as earthquakes, floods and catastrophes. They are anxious concerning offending God as well as fret over the tiniest of mistakes. They regularly spend their sources on calming incorrect gods and try to buy magnificent true blessings. Christianity, nevertheless, has an actual message of hope for all of these people that are plagued by superstition: Do not be afraid and be of cheer.

In this pre-season of Xmas that we call Development, we need to constantly pray for the world to be open to Christ's message of goodwill, mercy, as well as peace. Jesus has the prospective to conserve the entire planet from its anxieties and also to adoringly recover every person to God's support and also true blessings. If only Work knew back after that what we know now, he would never ever have been driven to anguish via his anxiety of God. He can have been comforted, accepted, and also motivated by God through the living presence of Jesus Christ in his life.

Prayer: *Lord Jesus, most of us carry hopes and fears in our hearts and also minds. We pray that You will certainly decrease our stress and anxieties by happily replying to our issues. Guard us as well as lead us. Welcome us as well as honor us. In Your Holy Name, we confidently hope. Amen.*

**Back to Contents**

9 – Christmas Sing-a-long

Hosea 6:3   "Let us recognize the LORD and sustain our knowledge of Him. He will appear just as the sun rises. Just like the rains in winter and those of spring that water the planet, He will come to us."

Right now of year, I normally tune my car radio to a station that plays Xmas songs all day for the month of December. I such as the old familiar festive tracks that I matured with. The majority of early mornings, you'll discover me lulling to Bing Crosby, Ella Fitzgerald, Nat King Cole, and also Andy Williams as I drive to church. The tunes get me in a terrific state of mind as well as even when interstate website traffic is slow, I simply enjoy even more time to sing along with my favored performers.

Christmas is all over me on my journey. I see cheery signs, Xmas trees, and seasonal sales everywhere. I poke fun at several of the signboards and also smile at church notices. I view people hurry and also scoot over at the shopping center. I even have a kid's pleasure when I see bright tinted Christmas lights as well as grass decors in subdivisions as I head back house in the evening.

I enjoy this time around of year, but I additionally remember that Christmas has not come yet, which this is really the sacred time of Development, when Christians anywhere are meant to be focused on the Second Coming of Christ. I contemplate quietly as well as wonder if I am gotten ready for that remarkable event. I turn off the Christmas music as well as switch on my heart to pray.

Will Christ return to Earth this year?

Prayer: *Lord Jesus, maybe You also delight in the brilliant lights, liveliness, as well as festivity of Christmas. People everywhere show up to like this time around of year for various reasons. We wish and also hope that they will certainly additionally quietly stop to think about You, Your Training, Your Life, as well as particularly Your Return. In Your Holy Name, we hope. Amen.*

Back to Contents

Isaiah 9:6   A child is born to us; a son is given. He will have all authority and power and will be known as the Wonderful Counselor, Almighty God, Eternal Father and Peaceful Prince.

The closer I reach Christmas, the even more pressure I place on myself. I normally feel as though the year has sped past too promptly and also I desire that the Lord would certainly insinuate an additional month between

Thanksgiving and also Introduction, simply to let me catch my breath.

And after that I re-read this stunning knowledgeable from Isaiah as well as comfortably breathe out. Xmas isn't regarding what I do, or what the church does; it's all about what God has done and also will do again. The actual company of the holiday comes from the King of Kings.

If we're under stress and burnt out, God provides a Terrific Therapist.

If we're weak or feeling tired, we can concern Almighty God.

With all of these marvelous qualities and attributes of God, we can all be really looking forward to spending Christmas with Christ.

Prayer: Lord Jesus, You are all that we require, particularly right now of year. Prepare our hearts and also minds to get You gladly, cheerfully, as well as consistently in our churches, our residences, as well as our hearts. In Your Terrific Name, we pray. Amen.

Back to Contents

11 – Salvationists

Luke 3:6 And all humanity will see the salvation of God.

When I was a young adult in Scotland, I worshipped with the Redemption Army. My friend at the time, George, had actually signed up with the Salvationists and also was an excellent cornet gamer. He always appeared to have an excellent mindset, was very dependable as a close friend, and also strove at college. I intended to resemble that, so I went to the Military Hall for a number of Sunday early morning conferences.

I suched as seeing the worshippers in their uniforms and also the worship was impressive. The individuals sang enthusiastically and the brass band played along. It was a remarkable experience and I wanted to become part of their area, yet to do so I needed to sign the pledge as well as I just had not been prepared to do that at the time.

I think I wished to have my cake as well as consume it, or to put it one more method, I wished to have my beer and drink it. Ultimately, I quit going to services because I knew I was being a hypocrite. It never ever affected George's relationship with me. If he was let down, I never ever understood it. He was a true Christian and years later on, when I increasingly battled against alcohol and battled with my faith, George's instance kept me going at times. I could see God's redemption in him when I was a young adult which aided me look for Christ later on in my life.

Introduction is a time when we can discover Christ. We frequently think about Him as the divine child in the precious manger, but also for those of us who have fought with life, He is much more than a Xmas card baby. Christ is the Hero of our hearts. He is the Chosen One in whom God's redemption can be seen by the entire globe.

If you're presently dealing with issues in your life and you're feeling insecure, after that please concerned Jesus and also get His complete confidence. He has actually assured us that He will certainly assist to carry our problems as well as recover us to God's merciful love. It's a remarkable true blessing and also a remarkable chance for salvation.

Prayer Lord Jesus, thanks for real Christians in our lives, whose personalities and also conduct attract us to God's salvation. Honor them for their understanding and also support. Bring us closer to You via God's amazing love. In Your Holy Name, we hope. Amen..

Back to Contents

12 – Expectantly Waiting

Luke 3:15 The crowds were hopefully expecting the coming of the
Messiah, so they wondered if John was actually the Christ.

I wonder what would certainly happen if we were to commemorate Introduction on a daily basis? A lot of us just consider this season when we see the candles being lit in church on Sunday mornings. A few of us may also think that Development is the holy time of year when we wait for the infant Jesus to be symbolically birthed amongst us.

Yet Introduction is much more than candle lights as well as baby cribs. It's not regarding nostalgically looking back or presently really feeling joyful; it's all about expectantly expecting a fantastic event.

" Expecting what?" I can hear a few of you claim. Anticipating that remarkable day when Christ will return to the Planet in all of His glory, grandeur, and also power. You see Introduction is not concerning Christmas Day; it's about completion of Time.

We spend a lot of the Yuletide holidays singing carols, acquiring presents, and covering presents, that we have actually failed to remember to wait expectantly for Jesus. Don't get me incorrect, I enjoy every one of the lights and also decors, glitter and garlands, as well as the Christmas trees and cards; however they do not mirror what this crucial church period is everything about.

I often want that a person would create Development cards with a photo of Christ's 2nd Upcoming and these words inside: 'Are you ready for Christ to return?' Instead, we will all send out and also obtain ho-ho-ho Santa cards, or ones envisioned with snow covered churches and sparkling fir trees, which sadly lead our ideas far from the Coming Messiah as well as back to the commercialized manger.
So I think today's challenge is this: are you getting ready for Christmas or Development?
Prayer: Lord Jesus, we have largely forgotten what Development represents. We hectic ourselves with Xmas, rather than taking some time to keep in mind that You are coming again to entirely reconcile Development, bring an end to Time, and also to evaluate the Planet. Keep us mindful of Your Return as well as help us to wait expectantly each day. In Your Holy Name, we pray. Amen.

Back to Contents

13 - A Christmas Prayer for our Troops

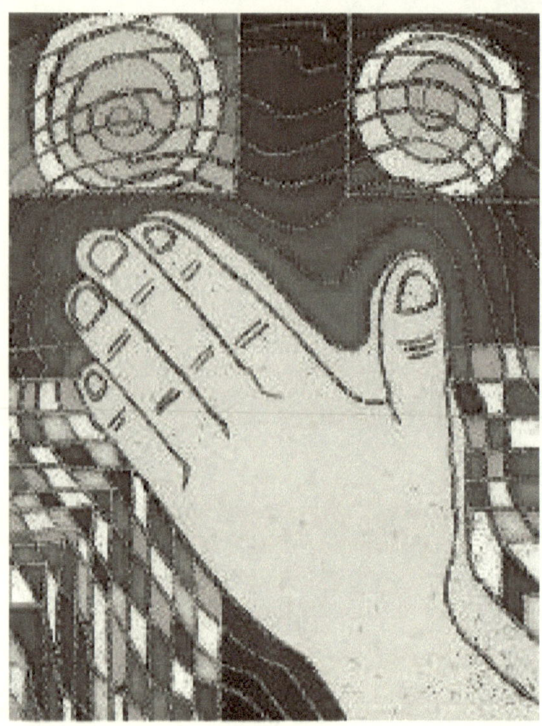

Today's devotion is a special prayer for those who are serving our nation overseas.

Almighty and also Everlasting God, as we celebrate the birth of Your Child in this globe and experience the peace He needs to supply us today, we remember our soldiers in the house as well as abroad who devote their lives to protecting our people on this earth.

We are sorry that war is still a component of our presence and that we call upon our young people to risk their lives for us, putting themselves in injury's way for our freedom. We pray that You will enable us someday to put an end to war and genuinely experience peace on Earth, to make sure that our future Development and Christmas parties will have plenty of delight.

We wish our soldiers pointed both here as well as abroad. We ask that You honor, shield and preserve them wherever they are located. Help us to allow them understand just how much we absolutely appreciate their service and give us chances to take care of, motivate, and also embrace them.

We wish their families that experience separation and distance currently of year. Border them with buddies as well as solid family members. Be near to the spouses, children and also mommies, hubbies, children, and dads who miss their enjoyed ones.

We likewise bear in mind those that have been wounded at work, who are recouping in the house or in Veterans' healthcare facilities. We wish their recovery, recovery, and also tender treatment. We specifically keep in mind those that are completely injured whether emotionally, mentally, physically, or neurologically. May they be deeply taken care of as well as fairly appreciated.

We wish our controling as well as army leaders that require to make challenging and unenviable decisions. We pray that You will certainly grant them advice as well as discernment to act on the fresh obstacles that threaten peace around the world.

Finally, we wish those service family members that have a vacant chair at their Xmas tables that will never ever be loaded. In the midst of their loss, border

them with caring good friends and caring individuals. Allow the real sacrifices that they have actually made, and still unfortunately experience, be humbly recognized and deeply appreciated by all. May we treasure the flexibility that our soldiers have achieved via the providing of their lives as well as accept them with our faith.

Hear us now as we quietly pray for those that serve our country today and also as we quietly keep in mind those that have actually proactively offered as well as compromised themselves in the past.
A time of silence
For the Holy One That made the Supreme Sacrifice for the world
-- Jesus Christ, our Lord as well as Rescuer. Amen

__Back to Contents__

14 – Double Decker Deliverance

Psalm 119:67 Prior to afflicting me, I wandered far from You; now I live by Your Word.

Believe it or otherwise, Psalm 119:65 -72 is my preferred scripture from the Old Testament. When I initially came to be a Christian in 1977, this passage had a remarkable affect on me as well as I have never forgotten what it implied for my life.

Someday I was resting on the top of a double-decker bus at the front seat. It was my favored position on the bus due to the fact that I constantly enjoyed the view it gave me of the city of Glasgow. As I travelled right into work, which took about 25 mins, I sometimes review from my Gideon's pocket edition of the Holy bible. These used to be provided to 5th grade classes in elementary school to every student before the days of political correctness.

Anyway, I was reading with the psalms back to back as well as reached Psalm
119. I really did not know that it had numerous knowledgeables in it, so I read it slowly section by area. When I reached knowledgeables 65-72, I felt as though God was speaking to my spirit, especially with verse 67: 'Before afflicting me, I strayed much from You; now I obey Your Word.'

You see, I understood that I had gone astray in my teenage life and also had actually as soon as turned down God. It was just when He afflicted my soul and also frequently bothered me emotionally that my life began to turn around totally. When I review those words for the very first time, I wanted to both weep and also laugh out loud, however being on a bus loaded with Glaswegians during the early morning rush hour stopped me in my tracks. Rather, I underscored those knowledgeables in my Bible as well as have maintained them written in my heart since.

We all roam from God at times and also ask yourself just how we'll ever return to being in a daily connection with Him. God might afflict our principles or our spirit relentlessly up until we have no option but to absolutely give up to Him. From experience, let me tell you that it is both humbling and terrific to lastly let God be God in life. He transformed mine in definitely amazing means; if you let Him this Arrival, I understand that He can do the same for you.

Prayer:O Lord, there are times when we roam from Your words and also enable ourselves to be sinfully seduced from Your Child. We appear to divide our hearts from Your Presence and range our spirits from Your impact. But You non-stop pursue us as well as afflict us constantly with Your loving, patient methods. Grant us the courage and also the will to reverse to Your Son, to make sure that we might be brought back to Your long lasting love. In Christ's Holy Name, we humbly hope. Amen

<u>***Back to Contents***</u>

Psalm 119:50   *In the midst of my suffering, I find comfort in this: my life is preserved through Your promises.*

Christmas can be a tough time for people who have actually lost their liked ones to death, especially if their loss happens during the month of December. I can remember when my very own Daddy passed away in December of 2002. It was in the middle of all the preparations for Christmas and my heart sank due to my loss. I saw every one of the decorations as well as listened to all of the carols, yet my heart might not experience a lot of the happiness. It was a sad time of year for me as well as even though years have actually passed considering that his fatality, I still feel part of that pain at Xmas.

Nonetheless, like the psalmist of old, I likewise feel the comfort God offers us through His assurances. Death does not have the final word as well as, with the shared hope of belief in Jesus Christ, my losses turn into victories as well as my grief can be changed right into gladness.

I understand that the feelings of despair are still there, however as time goes by, they are slowly being changed with a fullness of Christ's love that can conquer any kind of joylessness I may momentarily really feel. Jesus is born within me each Christmas, so I restore as well as rededicate my life, my enjoyed ones, as well as likewise my losses to Him. Jesus is my Comforter and Hero, Hope Bringer and Therapist, in addition to my Guard and also Lord.

Prayer: Lord Jesus, some of us are experiencing sad times and also our hearts are heavy due to the losses that we still experience. We understand that You weep with us and carry our cares. Help us to position our discomfort right into Your palms as well as permit us to offer over our emptiness to Your full accept. In Your Holy Name, we hope. Amen

<u>**Back to Contents**</u>

Xmas can be an unpleasant and lonesome time for some people. At our annual candlelight solution, we light a Blue Christmas candle for those who are grieving, harming, ill or alone during the joyful period. This prayer rhyme is stated as the blue candle light is lit. It's a really significant and also psychological time for some members in the churchgoers.

Blue Christmas Prayer

There's no area at Christmas for sadness,
There's no location for hearts that are blue.
All the globe intends to listen to Is a word full of cheer,
Not a sigh, not a tear, not from you.

There's no space at Christmas for loneliness,
There's no location for your emptiness and also sorrow.
All the world wants is peace,
Mistletoe as well as Christmas trees,
Not a heartache that mars its beliefs.

There's no area at Christmas for sickness,
There's no location or time to be ill.
All the world desires is wellness,
Prosperity and also wealth,
Not a discomfort that can spoil its goodwill.

There's no area at Xmas for Jesus,
There's no area for His household, also,
All the world would certainly not share,
Not a space going extra;
A steady would certainly simply have to do.

Silence ... ...
Yes, there's space at Christmas for unhappiness,
There's a location in God's heart for you.
For He knows pain and also loss,
Which He felt on the Cross,
So this candle light is lit here for you ...
* For God understands what it resembles to be blue.

 * *light a blue candle*

<u>Back to Contents</u>

17 – Still Amazed

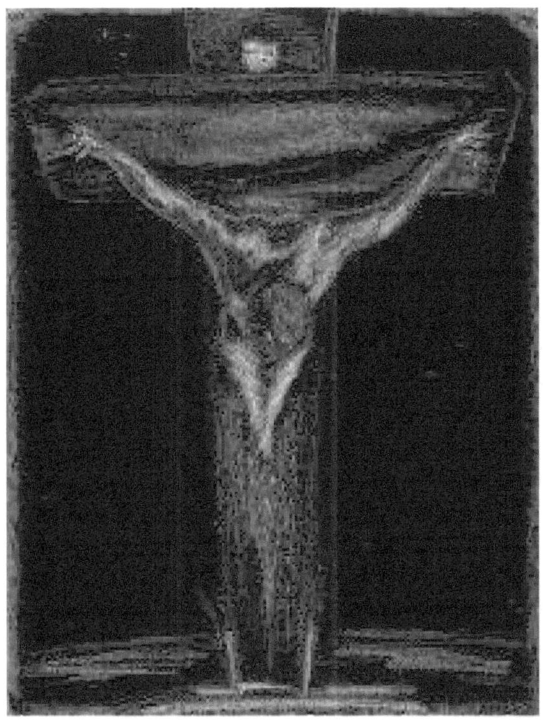

Psalm 66: 5 Come and behold God's great accomplishments; His deeds on our behalf are truly amazing!

John Calvin defined them as 'the attestations of God's witness to the globe.' Today we would certainly call them all-natural marvels, magnificent treatments, or perhaps fantastic escapes.

Among the obstacles that Christians have in this world is exactly how to reveal other

individuals where God is actually present as well as working in their lives. Skeptics tend to assume that we mentally sugar layer the truth as well as put on Rose of Sharon colored glasses. To others, it seems as though we are stubbornly holding on a two thousand years of age belief, which has actually participated in the realm of religious misconception and produced myth for contemporary beings. The globe of Wii, Guitar Hero, Twitter, as well as Facebook has no demand for lovely parables or a dreadful Scripture where blood and also rips, damaged limbs and bread retrieve the world. If God has any kind of 'awesomeness' delegated impress upon the here and now generation, after that He would certainly much better do it through cyberspace, ipods, and also anime. A sacred text is no more required, however a worthless capacity to message while multi-tasking would certainly be a significant plus.

And yet sunups and also sunsets still attract us. Marvelous mountains and also the greenest of valleys captivate our spirits. Christmas still touches something good even within the least religious amongst us, and also Easter each year fills us with brand-new life, clean slates, and also brand-new wonders.

We may become distracted by the newest gizmos and also be consumed with the most up to date patterns, but God still strolls and works amongst us, testifying to Himself in one of the most prevalent of all-natural occasions-- the hearing of birdsong in the quiet of the early morning, the rippling rhythm of a mountain stream, or the hurrying of waves crashing on craggy rocks-- they all witness to the power and glory, creative thinking and task of a God who still cares for His Production and also who seeks to recover a busted world.

Prayer: Lord Jesus, we call You the Son of God because Your words and methods reveal to us the elegance, peace, and also love of God. We look for those magnificent blessings in each of our lives, for we seek happiness and also satisfaction, contentment as well as harmony for our spirits. Instead of being agitated, help us to be relaxing. Rather than being sidetracked by points, assist us to end up being drawn in to confidence. Rather than constantly doing something imaginative, enable us to come to be developed beings. In Your Divine Name, we pray. Amen

Back to Contents

18 – Joseph's Courage

Matthew 1:20 While he was considering this, an angel of the Lord came to Joseph in a dream, saying " Joseph, Son of David, do not be anxious about taking Mary home to be your wife. The child within her has been conceived from the Holy Spirit."

Joseph had a hard option to make. He either had to employ in God's service as well as become Mary's protector because she was expecting, or he might have easily chosen to abandon her totally. It was a not a very easy situation and also his own online reputation went to stake. At one factor, he considered breaking the engagement independently, with no public spectacle. This would have brought little damage to himself as well as, at the same time, it would certainly have saved Mary from being stoned to fatality by a mad mob.

Before Joseph could accomplish this strategy, an angel visits him in a dream. The angel informs Joseph that the youngster will certainly be called Jesus which means Rescuer, Deliverer, and also Liberator all rolled into one. The stakes were currently higher than previously since Joseph was no longer expected to look after Mary as well as her kid youngster: the whole nation of Israel currently relied on his approval of his crucial role as other half, protector, and surrogate daddy.

I utilized to ask yourself why God really did not take control Himself, to start with by casting Joseph aside and after that surrounding Mary and Jesus with countless angels to secure them. Why did God provide Joseph the chance to do something that He could easily have done with His Almighty power?

Then it dawned on me. God operates in strange as well as poetical means. All of it returns to the Garden of Eden. Eve created mankind to fall into transgression by at first yielding to lure. When Mary accepted God's kid Jesus in her womb, I believe Eve's transgression was eliminated and God can start the last stage of compensatory woman-kind.

Adam's wrong was not a lot that he approved the prohibited fruit from Eve in the yard, yet that he failed to shield her from the snake and also morally abandoned her. So when Joseph approved the duty of protecting Mary and also Jesus, Adam's transgression of abandoning his spouse Eve was eliminated and also God commences the last stage in compensatory man-kind. It's what I call gender redemption. I presume God could call it the harmonizing of background, and also the total reconciliation of human-kind.

Christmas is only a week away and also when we gather with our friends and families, we will keep in mind Mary's Child Youngster with every one of the love and love that we can muster up. Yet allow's likewise require time to keep in mind Christ's Earthly parents as well as just how their choices to accept God's will certainly changed the world as well as conserved our lives. Their commitment to one another and their dedication to bring God's kid into the world; their nerve despite humiliation and also shame; their belief in God's word as well as His pledges are wonderful instances of just how easy, lowly individuals can aspire to conquer their conditions, by using the worthy features of responsibility as well as responsibility, devotion as well as respectability to make a lasting difference to their alarming circumstance and to the lives of all those around them.

Prayer Lord God we thank You for the blessings of our salvation through Jesus Christ, Your Divine Child. We are likewise thankful to Mary as well as Joseph for approving their duties as parents to Jesus that would restore everlasting hope to the entire globe. Thanks for choosing them and we also thank You for conserving us. In Christ's Name, we pray. Amen.

Back to Contents

Hebrews 7:25 Christ completely saves those who come to God through Him, because He intercedes for them always.

Occasionally, in the midst of all the stress that we put ourselves under, we reserved the factor for the season as well as get overtaken the monster of the Banquet. It behaves to buy points for individuals that we enjoy (as well as it assists the economic climate), but if we come to be as well stressed concerning just how we are clothed, or over- wrought with what we've gotten, we have actually missed out on the heart from the actual beginning, and made a mess of Xmas.

You see Xmas is not regarding what we're offering, however that we are forgiven. We try to find joy and happiness in all the incorrect places; we seek contentment as well as complete satisfaction in things that we will at some point throw out. We go on a Yuletide objective to remain pleased and rejoice, also when our hearts are breaking, as well as the demands that we position upon ourselves, and also those around us, have the prospective to demonize our spirits.

Christmas is implied to be kept merely in our hearts. I presume if God desired it to be a time of partying, there would have been plenty of area at the Bethlehem inn. Reveling is different from rejoicing. Indulging is not the same as worshiping. The tinsel and the shine, the toys and also the garlands are all decorations of our very own production. We will take them to save in a few days; Xmas will more than, however will we have missed the Christ?

Jesus will certainly still be functioning and also interceding for us in paradise. We depend upon Him daily to recover us to God. We might celebrate a million Xmases, shop in a billion shops, as well as hand out a zillion presents, but none of it would matter in infinite terms. If we do not pertain to God through Jesus, we can not be totally conserved. If we fail to provide our hearts and also lives to Him, Christ can not intercede on our behalf.

So allow's all make as well as take some time to set Christmas aside and also bring Christ to the front. Bear in mind, it's not regarding what we're providing or getting, it's about not neglecting what Christ is regularly flexible.

Prayer Lord Jesus, we seek to satisfy You quickly as a Star Kid, who is shaken delicately to oversleep a young mommy's arms, in the middle of a steady. We paint a Christmas card picture of the Nativity in our hearts and also minds, wrongly believing that this is all You call for of us. Transform us away from the quaint custom-mades of Christmas and also lead us towards You as our Christ. In Your Divine Name, we humbly pray. Amen.
Back to Material

Back to Contents

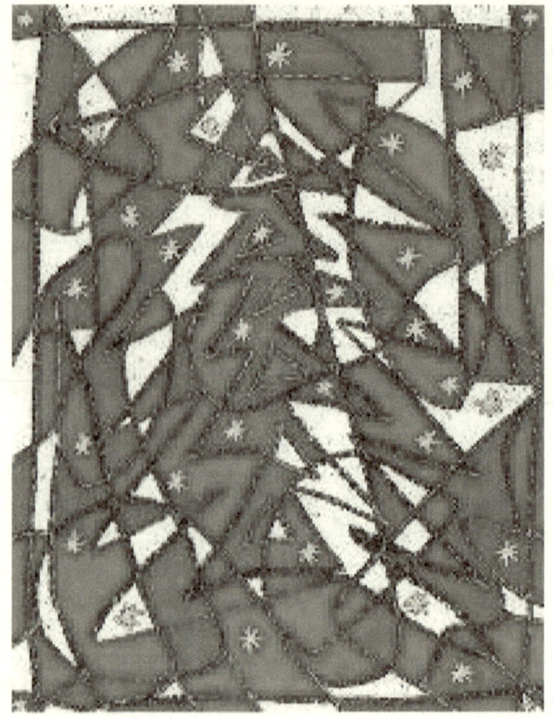

Matthew 7:11 Even those among us who are evil give good gifts to their children, therefore how much more will our Heavenly Father give gifts of goodness to those who ask of Him?

Probably, most of us are presently getting caught up with the hype of Christmas. We may have lists to check twice and stores still to shop. We may have been searching online for gifts and are now getting things delivered to our home. We do this because we all want to buy something nice for our families and friends, so that we can enjoy watching them being glad as they receive our gifts. It's the "Wow!" factor that we're looking for in a gift. We want to feel as though we've chosen the perfect gift, the best gift, the most wonderful gift ever for each of the loved ones in our lives.

And yet, no matter how pretty we make the bows, choose the wrapping, or pay for these gifts, they only last a little while. There's no gift that can last forever, despite what the merchants and manufacturers may tell us. All of the gifts that are given and received during Christmas of this year will eventually fade, fail, and turn to dust. Most of them will end up in a charity store at some time. And in the end all of them will become part of a landfill, never to be remembered, repaired or replayed.

This Christmas, as well as giving gifts, let's take time to write letters or cards to go along with them which tell the story of Christ and express our faith in Jesus. For no matter what or how much we give, a Gospel message is the greatest gift that we can present to all whom we love.

Prayer: Lord Jesus, this is the sacred time of Your everlasting joy when all the Earth proclaims Your Holy Coming. This Christmas help us to let others know who You are in our lives and how much Your love means to us. Perhaps, Lord, if we are sincere and genuine about expressing our faith, then that same, simple and everlasting gift of the Gospel will take hold in their hearts, too. In Your Holy Name, we pray. Amen.

Back to Contents

21 – Divine Separation

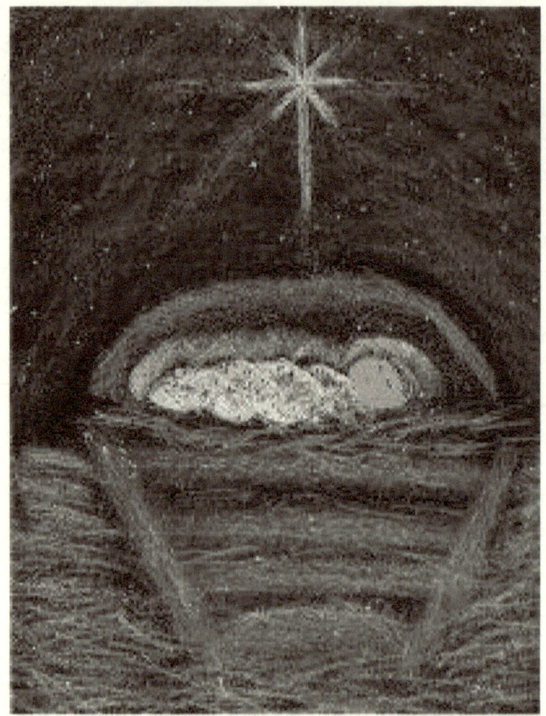

Psalm 113:5, 6 To whom shall we compare the LORD our God? He is the One enthroned in heaven, who looks down on Earth and the heavens.

I find Christmas absolutely amazing. And it's not just because of the great music, the beautiful lights, or the glorious glitter. I find it amazing because it's a celebration about the Lord of All Creation stooping down to our level, to leave His Holy Son amongst us. The whole event is a commemoration of an amazing sacrifice made by God.

What God did way back then would be like me taking my daughters, when they were babies, and leaving them on the streets of Mumbai. I couldn't ever do it because my fatherly love would not want to abandon them and I would feel the need to protect them. And that's precisely what makes Christmas so wonderful to me, when I realize how much love God truly has for the whole world that He was willing to let go of Jesus.

Years ago, when I first came to live in the United States, my eldest daughter Lynsey went to her first overnight camp. We were just in Knoxville about ten days and felt totally cut off from our families back in Scotland. We were on our own and it just didn't seem right that our eldest would be spending time away from us so soon. Lynsey felt the same separation anxiety and just after midnight I had to go and bring her home.

We were emotionally exhausted and weary as we journeyed home. I didn't know it, but I was driving on the wrong side of the road. Suddenly, I saw headlights in front of me and heard the blaring of a car horn. Seconds later, we were involved in a head-on collision. Thankfully, no one was injured but Lynsey and I were both emotional wrecks for months.

These days, Lynsey is a Residential Director of a college that is situated more than 1500 miles from home. We may be separated geographically, but we are still very close. This makes me wonder if that's the kind of relationship God maintained with Jesus throughout His life. God may have let Christ go to Earth that First Christmas, but They still carried each other in their hearts.

As I stated before, Christmas is amazing. And each year, I like to believe that God and Jesus stoop down to look at the Earth and celebrate this grand season with us.

Prayer: Lord God, most of us cannot comprehend what it took You to let go of Your Holy Son and leave Him to the mercies of the world. Even though You loved Him dearly, You never protected Him from what the world and people like ourselves eventually did to Him. That level of love and sacrifice is amazing to us and we are truly thankful for Your commitment which brought us salvation. In Jesus' Holy Name, we humbly pray. Amen.

__Back to Contents__

Psalm 65:8 Even those who live far away are amazed by Your wonderful deeds; when dawn breaks and twilight descends, You cause joyous songs to be sung.

Watching the news one December, I saw the unveiling of an atheist declaration of unbelief that was placed next to a menorah and a nativity scene. I can't remember in which city this occurred, but I couldn't help feeling sorry for the people who demanded that their own non-religious beliefs be put next to symbols and images of Hannukah and Christmas.

I guess it made them feel happy and that their own dignity was preserved. However, their statements about myths and no gods were ignored by the people who came to see the baby Jesus in the manger. They only had eyes for a good old fashioned nativity scene and for the feelings that it invoked. If anything, the atheistic declaration only heightened the spiritual awareness that God exists, and that our Redeemer came into the world 2000 years ago.

It makes me wonder what atheists fear about Christmas. Do they revel in their own misery rather than rejoicing in the mystery of God? Are they expecting folks to go around and be fearful, instead of encouraging others to come and be faithful? No matter what they think they have achieved in that city mall, the sounds of hope and laughter, mixed with carols and songs of joy, will continually be heard across the world each day till the end of Time.

No matter what the atheists in our society believe or don't believe, Christ is still the King of Christmas, and always will be throughout eternity.

Prayer: Lord Jesus, we thank You for the laughter and joy we experience each Christmas. We praise You for the warmth of Your Spirit and the wonder of Your birth. We welcome You into our hearts and homes, our towns and cities, our meeting places and shopping malls. Gloria in Excelsis! Amen.

Back to Contents

23 – Loving Neighbors

Romans 13:10 Love is not harmful to a neighbor, therefore Love itself fulfills the Law.

Our family grew up in what was known as an inter-war house in Glasgow, Scotland, which meant that it was built between 1919-1939. It's hard to describe because I've never seen anything like it over here in the United States. It was a large bungalow where four families lived. Two families, like my own, lived downstairs with front doors and small gardens. The other two families lived upstairs with side doors and side gardens. Everyone shared the massive backyard, which was usually used as a common area for drying the laundry on clothes lines. Needless to say, everyone lived in close proximity and as our family was the only one with kids in the building, we got into a lot of trouble from our neighbors for being too loud, too boisterous, and too wild.

One particular neighbor seemed to hate my sisters and brothers because she was always scolding us. She never smiled and was constantly criticizing my mom, who was doing her best to raise six kids. Eventually, because of all the pressure from this neighbor, my mother cracked one day and went absolutely crazy throwing things all around the house, while cursing loudly to the ceiling. I was there at the time and thought that my mom was going to kill the woman upstairs. That's when her mental illness seemed to start and, to this date, it has been the saddest day of my life.

For most of my teenage years, I found it hard to trust or respect any of my neighbors. I thought that the upstairs family had caused my mother's nervous breakdown. It was only years later that I finally realized she had been suffering from schizophrenia ever since she was a troubled teenager. All that my neighbor did was bring her mental condition to the surface. No one was really to blame. It just happened.

As Christians, we are called to be good neighbors, but in these days of privacy and seclusion, we're all making it very hard for people to get to know one another. Maybe that's why we feel lonely and vulnerable at times. Perhaps as we isolate ourselves and do our own thing, we're losing our connections with real people, real neighbors, and real home owners next door.

So on Christmas Day, I'm going to try, if the weather allows it, to sit on my front porch and say "Hi" to my neighbors. I guess if Jesus could leave heaven and be on the front porch of humanity, I should try to do the same. Who knows, perhaps then I might just experience the real meaning of Christmas.

Prayer: Lord Jesus, we all talk about being good neighbors but we don't really practice it. We all would like to live in a world where people greet each other and share peace with one another, but we don't want it to start with us. Help us to overcome our shyness and enable us to reach out to those around us, who are our neighbors and who are also God's children. In Your Holy Name, we pray. Amen.

Back to Contents

24 – Simply Serving

Psalm 84:10 It is better to spend a day in Your presence, O Lord, than a thousand in other places. I would choose to be an usher in God's house rather than be where wickedness abides.

I love this verse from the Psalms because it reminds all of us that the position of humility in God's service is far more precious than any fame or fortune. Whatever we do for the church, we do because we love God and want to minister to others, so that they will also be attracted into serving God.

As we draw near to Christmas, we are all humbled and touched by the simplicity of Christ's entrance into the world. He didn't come to Earth surrounded by thousands of angels and glorified by rulers from all over the world. He wasn't born into a family esteemed by riches and made prosperous by power. His first abode was a wooden shack, usually reserved for animals. His life was endangered almost immediately by King Herod, and his family became refugees for a while. Rather than being recognized as the King of kings and Lord of lords, he was just a mere baby, unprotected and vulnerable, with no power or authority.

This is why serving the Lord at church should never be something that we undertake in order to fulfill our ambitions, or build up our esteem. We serve the Lord because we are His servants. He calls and expects us to humbly do His will. He wants us to fulfill His ministries and missions, as opposed to completing our own dreams and desires. On Christmas Eve, we come as sinners saved by grace and as servants seeking to please our Sovereign.

Prayer: Lord Jesus, we proclaim You as our King. Help us to recognize and accept that we serve You, so that You alone will be honored and glorified. Give us the heart of a humble servant and encourage us to attract others to serve You faithfully, too. In Your Holy Name, we pray. Amen.

Back to Contents

2 Corinthians 3:17 The Lord and the Spirit are the same; freedom is experienced wherever the Lord's Spirit abides.

Last year, we had one of the best Christmas Eve services at the church where I serve as pastor. Families flocked to the church and filled the place with gladness and goodwill. The singing was tremendous and, as one person told me afterwards, when the congregation started with "O Come All Ye Faithful," it was overwhelmingly full of faith and joy. I think everyone in the service would have given the angels on the hillsides of Bethlehem a hard act to follow.

People felt free to express their faith through the wonderful music and traditional carols. The large amount of families and young children who attended the service brought a lot of pride and joy to my heart. That very morning, many of the youngsters performed their simple Nativity play, which brought a lump to our throats and tears to our eyes. It was just a perfect way to begin Christmas. It was just a beautiful time to rejoice in the Lord.

We live in a wonderful country. It isn't perfect by any means, but the people here truly understand what it means to be free. I personally think that having faith in Jesus and being empowered by the Holy Spirit are what sustains this freedom. I'm not saying that we're better or superior to everyone else. I'm not stating that we're more holy and saintly than any other country. I just believe that the true mixture of faith and freedom that we presently experience can only be encountered by truly rejoicing in Jesus.

That's what I experienced on Christmas Eve at the church, and everyone else seemed to feel the same. I hope and pray that we can carry the same Spirit within us each and every day until Christmas rolls around again next year. Perhaps if we can all succeed at that, peace and joy may spread across the Earth at last.

Prayer: Lord Jesus, thank You for a truly meaningful Advent season and enjoyable Christmastide. May the presence and experience of Your Holy Spirit reign in our hearts and minds. Help us to share what we have experienced of heaven in worship and prayer, with all whom we encounter each day on Earth. In Your Holy and Sacred Name, we pray. Amen.

__Back to Contents__

26 – Looking Ahead

Psalm 20:4 may God bless your heart's desire and bring success to all your plans.

After Christmas, there is always that in-between time when we all reflect about what's happened throughout the year, and then anxiously anticipate what lies ahead of us. We may get nostalgic or melancholy, depending upon what has occurred throughout the last twelve months. We may also be fearful and uncertain about the New Year.

Throughout this limbo of a time, I like to look at different Bible verses to see if I can come up with a motto for myself and the church that I serve. I was taught this by a ministerial friend in Scotland, who served his parish faithfully and pastorally. At the beginning of each year, he found a special verse and encouraged his congregation to embrace and apply it throughout the New Year.

Because I love the psalms, I tend to choose motto verses from the plethora of God's promises that are contained in that precious part of the Bible. The verse I have chosen for the readers of this book is Psalm 20 v 4. It's a promise from God that I have relied upon for many years. It reminds me that I am loved by God and my life is in His hands. It expresses help for the present and hope for the future. It makes me rely upon God as I serve His Son Jesus Christ with my life.

I hope that you can also experience the blessings of this Promise. I thank you for reading through this book and following this devotional journey during Advent. May the New Year be a blessing to you, your loved ones, and your church.

You can contact the author by email at the following address

pastor@erinpresbyterian.org

You can also view his artwork online at

www.stushieart.wordpress.com

if I can come up with a motto for myself and the church that I serve. I was taught this by a ministerial friend in Scotland, who served his parish faithfully and pastorally. At the beginning of each year, he found a special verse and encouraged his congregation to embrace and apply it throughout the New Year.

Because I love the psalms, I tend to choose motto verses from the plethora of God's promises that are contained in that precious part of the Bible. The verse I have chosen for the readers of this book is Psalm 20 v 4. It's a promise from God that I have relied upon for many years. It reminds me that I am loved by God and my life is in His hands. It expresses help for the present and hope for the future. It makes me rely upon God as I serve His Son Jesus Christ with my life.

I hope that you can also experience the blessings of this Promise. I thank you for reading through this book and following this devotional journey during Advent. May the New Year be a blessing to you, your loved ones, and your church.

You can contact the author by email at the following address

pastor@erinpresbyterian.org

You can also view his artwork online at

www.stushieart.wordpress.com